The Floorball Guru Primer

Principles & Dynamics of learning, developing, and coaching the world's fastest growing game.

By
David Crawford, M.S.,
Floorball Guru

Kirby Publishing, LLC
Lacey, WA 98503

ISBN 978-1-947863-03-3 (Paperback Black & White Interior Form)
ISBN 978-1-947863-05-7 (Paperback Color Interior Form)
ISBN 978-1-947863-04-0 (E-Book Form)

Library of Congress Control Number 2018953817

Book Design by Troy Kirby

Front cover image by Rodney Hiram

All graphs, charts, tables, illustrations, contributions, strategies and concepts listed in this book are copyright of David Crawford

Photos provided by Adam Troy: Founder of USA Floorball, currently on the board as executive director. Content producer and photographer for Swedish Floorball Club Storvreta IBK and IFU Arena.

Printed and bounced in the United States of America.
First printing August 2018.

Published by Kirby Publishing, LLC
Lacey, WA 98503

Visit www.floorballguru.com for more information

This book is dedicated to Heidi, Dylan & Logan,
Without them, this book may have never gotten off of the ground.

Table of Contents

Table of Contents

Foreword

About a year ago, David Crawford reached out to me on social media to ask if he could share an idea with me. I am all about engaging with community, and he was local, so we set up a time to meet. Prior to our meeting, he sent me a link to a sport he had been playing and coaching and introducing locally - FLOORBALL.

What?

I have been an athlete for 42 years. I have played basketball and soccer in 14 countries, softball in 10. I had taught physical education briefly in a middle school. I knew sports. I had never heard of Floorball.

When I met David later that week, he oozed with enthusiasm for Floorball. After watching videos and hearing about his own personal experience, I was intrigued. He let me know he would be hosting an open house with opportunities for the community to come out and learn the rules, to hold a stick, and play a game. I was in!

The day came, and I had so much fun! We practiced holding the [sticks] and shooting on goal. We scrimmaged with teams that spanned ages - from 4 to 54. I am not young anymore, but I wish I had heard of this sport in elementary school. I wish I could be one of the few who get to represent the United States of America when Floorball becomes an Olympic sport.

David is not only passionate about the sport. He is a teacher by trade and knows how to teach and coach others to play. He is committed to expanding opportunities. He has figured out ways for students from all communities, even those who lack resources, to be able to afford equipment. He communicates these ideas in a clear way and a style that is accessible.

This book is a must for every physical education teacher, for every YMCA director, for every Boys and Girls Club activities coordinator. Floorball is a sport that can be played and mastered by those who are already skilled athletes and those who are just looking for a way to stay moving. This is a sport that can bring together community and teach values that are so lacking in society today.

Erin Jones

former Assistant State Superintendent,

current Education Consultant.

Introduction

The focus of this book is to cover a variety of floorball-related topics to help you get started. Our focus is on giving you, the instructor, a foundation on which to build on. This is a guide for you to use, but we encourage you to add your own experience and knowledge to your program. Our focus is teaching you the basics while giving you the best platform to be successful.

Inside you will find explanations on the benefits of floorball and why this activity is the right choice for school physical education classes, city parks and recreation programs, university intramural sports, hockey organizations, and other sports-related organizations. By reading this you will gain a better understanding of floorball and a variety of skills to improve your instruction.

To provide a fun and safe learning atmosphere, all participants must have basic knowledge of the rules. Like many sports, floorball has a comprehensive rule book. While the rules are important to know and understand, we've simplified learning the game by focusing on teaching rules that will ensure the safety of the participants while maintaining the integrity of the game. In addition to the official game rules, teachers/instructors can also adapt some of the rules and gameplay to fit their specific needs and facility restrictions.

Floorball is a fun all-inclusive sport that can be adapted to facility, age of player, player ability, and quantity of players. Floorball does not have to be played as a traditional match sport; in fact, floorball can be played in numerous forms. We encourage you to be creative in how you present this sport.

As with other school subjects, physical education teachers rely on lesson planning to create beneficial lessons and units. In this curriculum, you as a physical education teacher/instructor will find all the information needed to conduct a fun, safe and beneficial floorball unit. You will find that drills and games from other sports can be used to teach floorball skills as well.

What Is Floorball?

Floorball looks like floor hockey, but varies in some key areas such as equipment used and rules of the game that make it ideal in a physical education setting. A floorball stick is composed of a fiberglass shaft with a plastic blade that does not damage gym floor surfaces. Floorball sticks are sized from around the belly versus the chin. A lighter shorter stick allows players more control of the ball, and of their sticks.

The format of floorball is like ice hockey, with two teams of five players facing off on the court. A traditional game can be played in three 20-minute periods or three 15-minute periods. The size of the court and the number of players can be modified based on your class size, gym space and overall needs. Not only is floorball safe and fun, the activity also promotes movement, team building and physical and social development.

History of Floorball

Floorball was developed in Sweden in the 1970's, but didn't initially gain much ground. Today, floorball is played by millions of people across the world (in 60+ countries) in various settings, including schools, teams and community programs. The introduction of floorball to the United States occurred in the early 1990's, when European players set up teams across the country. Today, floorball is growing in popularity across the United States in schools, organizations, and community settings.

Floorball Equipment Standards

Sticks: Floorball sticks come in various lengths and models, and are typically constructed of either fiberglass, carbon fiber, or a mixture of both. The blades are made of plastic. Most sticks come with a right or a left curve (right-handed versus left-handed players). If you look at most blades they will have a flat side (backhand), and concaved side (forehand). When purchasing sticks for your group, keep in mind Americans tend to be more right handed than left handed. A starting point would be 60/40 right to left, and your bulk stick purchase may reflect that for right and left-handed sticks.

Court/Space: Floorball can be played anywhere and on any surface. In some cases, a smaller gym might be better suited for your group than a large open gym. Note that asphalt and rough concrete will wear out the blades faster than gym floors and smooth concrete.

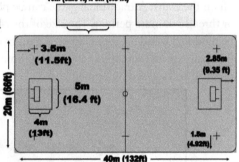

Eye Protection: While the rules of floorball help keep sticks down, things do happen and occasionally a stick will come up to the head; or a ball will fly into the air. Because of this, it is recommended that players wear eye protection. Eye protection is not required in floorball, but it won't hurt. Depending on your risk management for sports activities there may be a requirement for participants to wear eye protection. Eye protection can be as simple as racquetball googles.

Goals: Floorball uses specific goals, but in many cases, facilities can adapt current goals on hand. Groups can use smaller 2x3 foot goals or larger depending on the size of the group and need.

Ball: Floorballs are made of plastic and resemble outdoor pickle balls, but they are significantly stronger and more aerodynamic. There are 26 different holes in each ball, to decrease air resistance. A floorball weighs approximately 0.8 ounces and has a diameter of 2.8 inches.

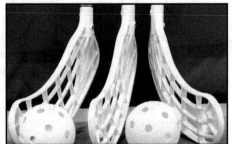

Floorball Equipment
Floorball Stick

In an instructional setting, it is important to take time to properly size the stick to the participant and ascertain whether the player is right-handed or left-handed.

When introducing this concept, some players may already know how they hold the stick; if not, there are a few tricks to quickly assess this in a larger group setting. The key is comfort for the player. They may assume they are right-handed, but may be more comfortable playing left-handed.

Have the player grab the stick. If their right hand is closest to the end of the stick the stick will fall to the left side of the body meaning they use a left-handed stick. Talk to the player and encourage them to find out what is most comfortable for them to play with.

If you're able, let players try both left-handed and right-handed sticks to find out what is most comfortable. While they may tell you one over the other, you may have to adjust sticks as needed. Remember, which side a player uses doesn't matter; what matters is that they're comfortable using the stick.

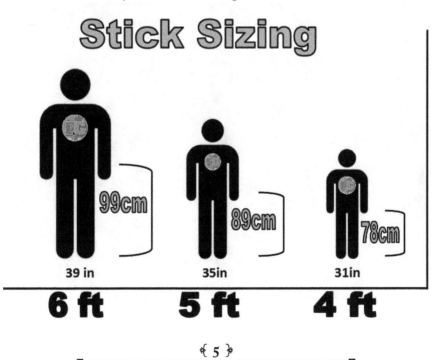

Stick Holding

Students should always be encouraged to hold the stick with two hands during drills and games. This is especially important while passing, shooting or controlling the ball in a static position. While one hand is permissible remind players that they must always have control of their stick.

The top hand should fall at the end of the shaft, farthest from the blade. This hand is considered the steering hand. The second-handed position will vary depending on comfort and whether the player is passing or shooting. As an instructor, what you want to look for is a player's hands that are close together, and make the necessary corrections.

If both hands are too close, it will minimize the player's ability to dribble, pass, and shoot. Encourage players to separate their hands along the grip and to take a more athletic stance.

Player Stance

Floorball sticks are shorter than hockey sticks. While hockey sticks are sized to the chin, floorball sticks are sized around the belly. This forces players into an athletic stance. Players should have their feet shoulder width apart with knees bent. They should be balanced, not leaning too far forward or backward. Hands should be separate along the shaft of the stick, but not together. If the player is standing up the hands will come together making them less effective when dribbling, shooting, and passing.

Other Aspects

1. Hold the stick with two hands as often as possible, particularly when passing, shooting, controlling the ball while standing still, or participating in drills.

2. If the player chooses to place the stick to the right of the body, the left hand must always be on top of the stick, and the right hand below. If the player chooses to place the stick to the left of the body, the right hand must always be on top and the left hand below.

3. During play encourage players to take a player's stance to promote proper form. Players should stand with their feet shoulder width apart with a slight bend at the knees to lower their hips and give them more stability. This will promote a slight forward lean, but they should not be using their stick to support their body.

Floorball Basics

This section will explain the basic techniques related to passing and shooting. In an instructional setting, the instructor should be focused on teaching proper techniques while giving corrective instruction as needed. To teach these skills, it is important to fully understand the basic technique to develop a better understanding of the game.

Passing & Receiving
Pass (Forehand)

When passing the ideal position of the ball is behind the body (rear foot). To start the pass, draw the blade across the ground towards the intended target. The ball should be released prior to the blade passing the front foot.

Instructional Keys

1. The pass should initially be practiced in a static setting.

2. Watch the release. If the ball is released beyond the front foot it will open the blade up sending the ball into the air.

3. Encourage players to rotate their palms down during a pass. This positions the blade down keeping the ball tight to the ground resulting in a smoother pass.

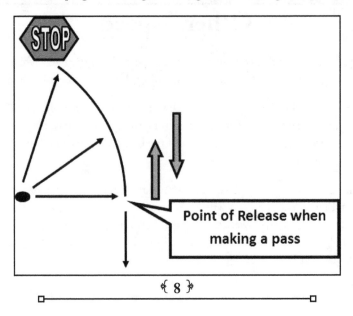

STOP

Point of Release when making a pass

Pass (Backhand)

Backhand passes can be performed in two ways, including a sweep or hit pass. The use of either pass will depend on the situation the player is presented with. The technique for a backhand pass is like the forehand. The main difference the change in body position. For a right-handed shooter, the hands will remain the same, but the stick will cross the body, resulting in the back of the player facing the intended target. This can be a difficult skill to learn in the beginning, but an effective one to learn.

Receiving a Pass

In an ideal world, every pass would be a good one. A good pass goes straight to the player with minimal or no bounce. Players should accept or cradle the ball by moving their stick with the ball until the point where they change the directional movement of the ball. Accepting or cradling the ball gives players the best opportunity to control the ball. Players should avoid creating a solid wall with their stick when receiving a pass; doing so will result in the ball bouncing off the stick, which makes it more difficult to control.

Instructional Keys

1. Many young players simply hit the ball during a pass instead of cradling it. You'll likely address this concept many times before it catches on.

2. Encourage players to stop the ball first before passing.

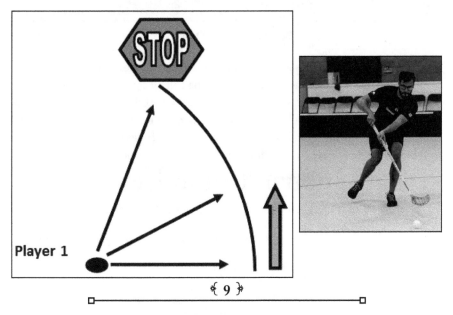

Shooting
Wrist Shot

The wrist shot is the most basic shot to learn. To complete a wrist shot the ball should be placed behind the body. During the follow-through players, will release the ball at or in front of the front foot. Initially, players, should strive to keep the ball on the ground then progress higher as they become comfortable with the shot.

Slap Shot

The slap shot is another shooting option. As the name implies, you're literally slapping the ball. Unlike a wrist shot, you hit the ball by approaching it from behind. The slap shot is about power, and generating that energy through the stick. To achieve that, players should look to contact the ground prior to hitting the ball. This flexes or loads the shot, and as the blade is dragged toward the ball, the energy will eventually be released upon contact in a sweeping motion forward.

Instructional Keys

1. Players should keep their palms down during the follow through.

2. Point the toe of the blade at the intended target during the follow-through.

3. Sticks must remain below the waist during the backswing and forward swing.

Dribbling

Dribbling is focused on controlling the ball by keeping it from the opposing team. The need to dribble will vary depending on the situation. Dribbling in floorball uses the same concept as dribbling in soccer and basketball. Players are encouraged to be comfortable using both sides of the blade to dribble the ball. When teaching new players, encourage them to start with two hands on the stick. Players may use one hand when dribbling, and many drills can help build their skills in these areas.

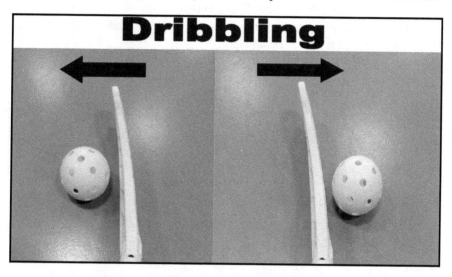

Instructional Keys

1. A light touch on the ball is key when dribbling.

2. Watch the hand and body position of players. A player with their hands close together is less effective when dribbling the ball.

3. Floorball sticks are shorter than hockey sticks. This forces players to have to bend their knees. The player shouldn't be standing straight up, or have their stick supporting their weight.

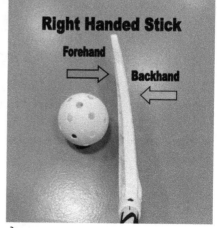

Floorball Activities

Games can be played 5v5, 4v4, or 3v3, and played with or without goalies. Ultimately this will be based on the number of players and the space that you have available to play in. One of the great things about floorball is that it's easily adaptable to the needs of the program. Whether you use a goalie or not, it is recommended that you create a goalie box. Players are not allowed in the goalie box, which will help keep players from fully blocking the goal, especially when using smaller goals. It's likely you will need to remind players of this rule, but it's a good idea to have some sort of visual reference. If you are unable to put tape down you can use lines on the court as needed.

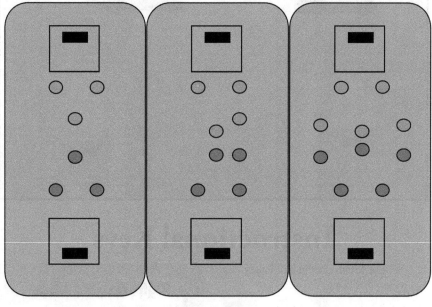

Drills

Drills come in a variety of shapes and sizes. It's recommended to avoid an instructional setting based solely on drills, particularly for younger or beginner players. The focus should be on learning and having fun, and while drills play a part in that, it can be done through play. Tag games and relay races are great ways to teach skills in a fun manner.

Instructional Keys

1. Pull from what you already know. What's great about sports is that a lot of times you can use the same drill across multiple sports. If needed you can adapt it, but in the end, it's still getting the point across.

2. Not every drill, game, or activity will be a hit. If it falls apart, regroup, cover basic rules of the game and give it another try. If it falls apart, move on, don't force a game or drill.

3. Have a few extra drills in mind in case you need them, or have a skill progression ready if your group outperforms expectations. Either way, be prepared to shift gears as needed.

4. Have fun with it, get inventive, and encourage your players to be creative. Players are typically already excited to play. Players standing around too much get bored.

Floorball Rules

Floorball, like many sports, has rules and regulations. While the rules are important to know in a recreational setting, when starting out, most of them aren't necessarily needed to enjoy the game.

High Stick: It is important to spend time emphasizing the importance of always maintaining control of their stick. The rules of floorball specifically state that the stick must not go above the waist. While it will happen, if the situation is not dangerous and a stick comes up too high, it's a good idea to give a verbal reminder, but stopping play isn't necessarily  required. During instruction, it is recommended to routinely remind and quiz players on this rule. The more they play, the less likely you'll have this problem. The picture above shows a player shooting the ball and allowing the follow through to go above the waist. This is allowed if there is not another player nearby. The focus here is to encourage developing players to always control their sticks. More importantly, emphasize safety.

Physical Contact: Overall there is little contact allowed, but it does happen. With younger players, you won't tend to see as much contact happening as with older players. As with soccer, players can shoulder their opponent when going for the ball. If you're playing with high school or college players, it's recommended to give reminders as needed. Players may not go through their opponent, or body check them off the ball. Both are considered fouls.

Stick Fouls: Floorball rules specifically prohibit players from hitting an opponent's stick. Players may not come down on or stick lift their opponents to win the ball. Players may also not go through an opponent's stick. There will always be minor, unintentional stick hitting when two or more players are fighting over the same ball. It will be important to distinguish between the two and to call fouls accordingly. In addition, players may not do the following

- Blocking or kicking an opponent's stick is not allowed.

- Lifting or purposely holding an opponent's stick is not allowed.

- Players are not allowed to place their stick, leg or foot in between an opponent's legs.

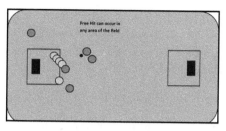

Free Hits: A free hit is basically the same as a free kick in soccer in that when a foul occurs, the ball leaves the field, or there's a stoppage of play a free hit is awarded. All free hits are direct plays meaning a player can either shoot, or pass. A free hit can happen at any time and anywhere on the court. If a foul occurs inside the goalie box, the free hit is moved nine feet from the box. Defensive players may set up a wall to defend a free hit, but must be nine feet from the ball- this includes the defending players' sticks.

Hit-In: A hit-in occurs when the ball leaves the playing surface. The ball is placed around the area where it left the field and play is resumed once the ball is played. If the offensive team plays the ball outside the field the ball is turned over to the other team. Another way to think of it is whoever touches the ball last when the ball goes out of bounds the ball is given to the other team. Think

of basketball and how turnovers occur when the ball leaves the field. It is the same thing for a hit-in.

Face-Off: Every time a game/period starts, or a goal has been scored, a face-off is taken at center court. Unlike in hockey, where the puck is dropped, the ball is placed on the floor as in lacrosse. One person from each team will vie for the face-off. Players place their sticks on opposing sides of the ball. The distance of the sticks to the ball should be close, but not touch the ball. Once the whistle blows, play is started.

Playing Area/Boundaries: Unless you can afford boards or have space to simulate a rink, it's likely that you'll be using some sort of line as a field barrier. In most cases instructors will be limited by space and other factors. Don't let that be a hindrance. Get creative with what you have.

Factors to consider when determining rink size:

- Age of the participants. Younger players will get more out of the game by playing in a smaller area. This will give them more opportunities to play the ball as opposed to chase it.

- Physical ability of the players. It is best to do some drills or activities to assess the abilities of your group.

- Number of participants. If needed you can play 3v3, 4v4, or 5v5. This also may depend on the number of sticks available.

- In looking at your space, what hazards are present that can or cannot be moved? What can you do to protect players from hitting potential hazards?

Having a rink is an added perk to the sport. It is not necessary to play, and often, schools can't afford the cost. In many cases schools have one or two gyms; or a multi-purpose room that will suffice. Look around, and you will find space to play that suit your needs.

Official-size goals are not required to play. In many cases, facilities will already have goals that can be adapted for a variety of scenarios. If you're using a larger goal you can use a shooting trainer as a stand-in for a goalie.

Guarding the Goal: If you are not using goalies the best way to avoid players camping in front of the goal is to place a small goal box around the goal. Players are not allowed in the box. If you have lines on a gym floor designate one of them as a reference point. It won't be perfect, but it will help.

Otherwise you can use tape. If you're outside use chalk to mark the goal box.

High Stick Rule: This is by far the most important rule for instructors to enforce. High sticks can lead to dangerous situations and may cause injuries. Drive home the point that players must always keep their sticks below their waist, including during shots, and they can't touch the ball with their stick above the knee. It is likely that you'll need to remind beginning players about this rule on a regular basis. It's a good idea to spend time reminding players each day/week of these safety rules.

We've covered a lot of information pertaining to Floorball, but we haven't even scratched the surface. Learning new things takes time so don't feel like to you must attack it all at once. As you being to play you'll start learning more each time. As you and your players develop you'll be able to take the next steps. The important thing is to play the game as designed and have fun. Everything else will come in time. As a new sport education is key and being able to effectively market this new venture will be a crucial component to raising awareness. Add Floorball into your current multi sports camp, after school program, recess offering, or off-ice training development. If it doesn't take off right away that's ok. Play the long game. As more and more people become aware of Floorball, the more it will grow. In the future, there's a real possibility that we'll see it evolve into a high school and collegiate varsity sport.

Floorball Unit Overview

The Floorball Guru unit consists of eight (8) lesson plans for introductory to intermediate Floorball instruction. This curriculum will lay out a plan to effectively teach Floorball in a controlled setting.

Each lesson consists of an introduction, a review of safety rules, learning objectives, drills, and a fun game.

Our lessons run for <u>45 to 60 minutes</u>.

Units can be modified to fit your needs and time restrictions.

Our focus is on providing an all-encompassing Floorball program that will benefit you (the instructor) and your players.

We realize that every teacher runs their classroom differently. While we encourage you to follow the lesson plans, you are more than welcome to adapt the curriculum to meet the needs and restrictions of your group and/or facility. The more you teach this program the more you'll be able to bring your own experience to the unit. This will only enhance the lesson and learning.

We hope that you'll learn something through this unit, and that, above all else you and your players will have fun.

Floorball Unit Template

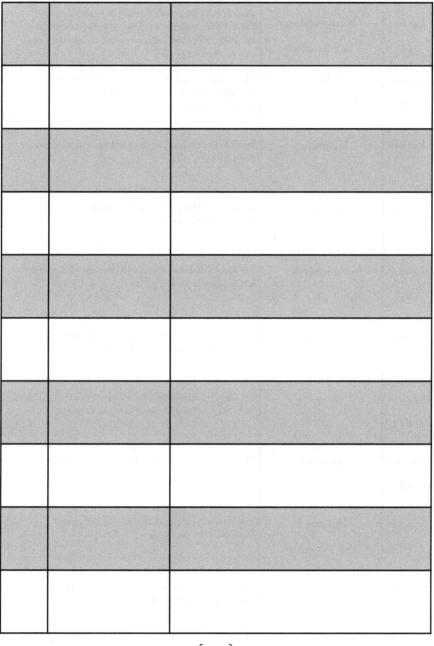

Floorball Curriculum

Lesson #1	Introduction To Floorball	Players will learn a basic history of Floorball in the U.S. Players will also learn basic techniques when holding the stick, dribbling, safety rules and an introduction to playing the sport.
Lesson #2	Dribbling #1	Players will learn basic techniques for dribbling the ball through various exercises and games using static and dynamic movement.
Lesson #3	Dribbling #2	Students will expand on their dribbling skills through drills with the ball.
Lesson #4	Passing	Students will learn basic techniques for passing and movement with the ball.
Lesson #5	Game Day #1	Students will use all of the skills learned so far through scrimmages and competitions.
Lesson #6	Shooting #1	Students will learn basic techniques for shooting the ball including learning a wrist shot and slap shot.
Lesson #7	Shooting #2	Students will expand on their shooting skills through drills focused on movement and quick release.
Lesson #8	Defense	Students will learn basic defensive techniques and tactics.
Lesson #9	Putting It All Together	Students will receive skills and lessons learned throughout the program.
Lesson #10	Game Day #2	Students will learn basic techniques for passing and movement with the ball.

Lesson 1

Introduction To Floorball

Students will learn the following in this lesson:

1. The basic concepts of the game of Floorball.

2. How to properly hold the stick, as well as correct player stance.

3. Basic dribbling skills along with safety rules pertaining to Floorball.

Instructor will observe students understand of key safety rules. Students should be able to show consistent control of their stick with minimal reminders from the instructor. This is shown by students keeping their sticks below the waist.

Assess the student understanding of the positive effects of playing floorball as well as the history of the sport in the United States. Observe student ability to hold the stick properly in a static position and dribbling the ball while moving.

Note: The instructor should familiarize themselves with the history of the game of Floorball, safety rules, the positive benefits associated with Floorball, and the basic techniques for holding the stick properly during gameplay.

Equipment needed:

- Sticks

- Balls

- Cones

Lesson 1 Breakdown

Lesson Segment	Time	Description
Program Intro	3 minutes	• Introduce yourself and do a roll call (if necessary). Give a brief introduction on Floorball. • Introduce what skills you will be covering for the day and give a basic run-down on how Floorball & floor hockey differ.
Safety Intro	3 minutes	• Introduce the stick. • Cover basic safety rules (stick heights below the waist and remind players to always have control of their sticks). • Introduce the whistle or commands you choose to give, and what it means when players hear it blown.
Holding The Stick	10 minutes	• Cover how to size the stick and how to know which stick is right or left. • Show how to properly hold the stick and proper athletic stance. • Demonstrate proper dribbling (static position), emphasizing light touches on the forehand/backhand.
Game / Exercise	15 minutes	• Large box dribbling • Zombie Attack
Scrimmage	15 minutes	• Introduce scrimmage including positions for offense and defense. • Introduce how to do proper face-offs.
Review / Closure	5 minutes	• Discuss today's lesson with the students.

Large Box Dribbling

Each participant is given a ball. The object is to practice stick handling while moving around within a designated space. The box can be as large as needed, or smaller to challenge or progress the activity. Players may run or walk while dribbling the ball. Emphasis should be placed on ball control and both hands on the stick. Encourage players to look up while they move to avoid other players.

Progression: On whistle command, players should speed up their movement, while saying in control.

Equipment needed: Sticks, Balls

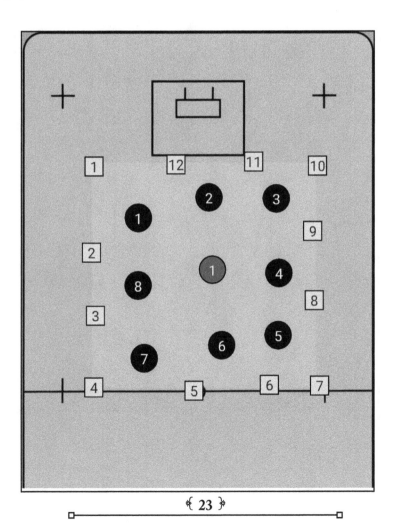

Zombie Attack

Each player has a ball, but the instructor doesn't have a ball. The object is for players to avoid turning into zombies, which occurs when their ball is stolen and put into a net. At this point the player becomes a zombie and helps turn other players into zombies. Remind players that they're not a zombie until their ball is in the net. Encourage them to recover their ball if they can. The game continues until all of the balls are in the net. This is a good time to remind players about stick control. It will introduce players to the concepts related to defensive play.

Equipment needed: Sticks, Balls, Goal

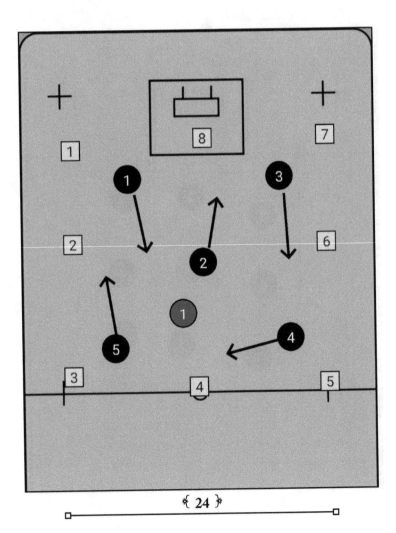

Lesson 2
Dribbling

Students will build on skills learned from Lesson 1. In this lesson, players will progress in their ability to properly hold and control both stick and ball.

The instructor will observe a student's ability to effectively control the ball in static and dynamic positions. This is shown by student's ability to keep sticks below the waist, and consistently control the ball.

Assess the student's understanding of the basic safety rules related to Floorball.

The instructor should continue to familiarize themselves with the safety rules. Instructors should also review how to properly dribble the ball.

Equipment needed: Sticks, Balls, Cones (or other line markings), & Hula Hoop/rope or something similar (to make a circle).

Lesson Objectives

Students will:

1. Consistently demonstrate proficiency in holding the stick properly (one hand on top and the other hand below).

2. Demonstrate proficiency in ability to control the ball in a static and dynamic position.

3. Demonstrate knowledge of safety rules.

Dribbling is a core component to success in Floorball. Make sure to spend time on this skill. Encourage players to rotate their wrists while tapping the ball instead of slapping at it. Get players to feel for the ball on their stick without looking at it. During match play, new players tend to hit the ball away instead of controlling and dribbling. Encourage players to control and dribble the ball first, before hitting or passing.

Lesson 2 Breakdown

Lesson Segment	Time	Description
Lesson Intro	2 minutes	• Introduce yourself and do a roll call (if necessary). Give a brief introduction on Floorball. • Introduce topics covered in this lesson.
Content Review	3 minutes	• Cover basic safety rules. • Remind players about necessary commands & whistle procedure. • Remind players about athletic stance and how to hold the stick.
Dribbling Exercise	5 minutes	• In a static position, run players through a variety of dribbling exercises. These are exercises they can practice at home. • Emphasize a light touch and keeping the stick/ball close.
Game / Exercise	10 minutes	• Planets.
Game / Exercise	10 minutes	• Stop, Go, Control.
Scrimmage	15 minutes	• Remind players about proper face-offs. • Emphasize player positions (offense/defense). • Introduce fouls/free-hit procedures.
Review/ Closure	5 minutes	• Discuss today's lesson with students.

Planets

Planets (shown below) Players are sorted into multiple teams (planets), given a home base. The goal is to collect as many satellites (balls) as possible. Astronauts must travel through space, collect (dribble) one satellite to take back to their planet. Satellites may be strewn across space and astronauts may need to travel farther away from their planet in order to collect satellites. Only one astronaut from each team may leave the planet at any time. The team with most satellites wins.

<u>**Equipment needed:**</u> Sticks, Balls, Cones, Pennies

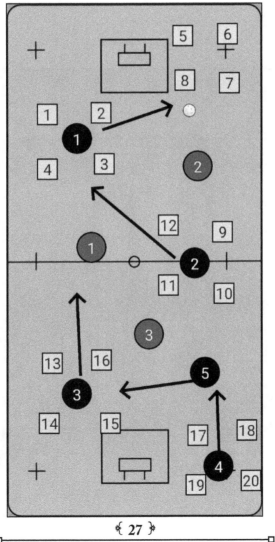

Stop, Go, Control

Players line up behind a predetermined line with a stick and ball. The instructor will say, "GO," and participants move as fast as possible toward the finish line. When the instructor says, "STOP," everyone should immediately stop moving. Players who are caught moving on a red light may be sent back to the starting line. This is at the discretion of the instructor. Players should focus on controlling and be ready to stop their ball immediately.

Equipment needed: Sticks, Balls, Cones (or other line markings).

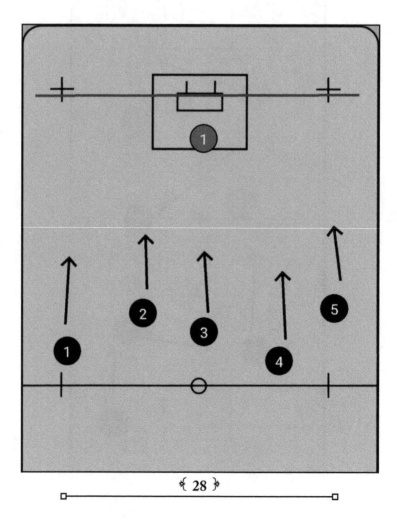

Lesson 3
Dribbling

Students will build on skills learned from Lesson 2. In this lesson players, will continue to progress in their ability to properly hold and control both stick and ball.

The instructor will observe a student's ability to effectively control the ball in static and dynamic positions. This is shown by a student's ability to keep sticks below the waist and consistently control the ball.

Assess the student understanding of the basic safety rules of Floorball.

The instructor should continue to familiarize himself or herself with the correct approach to hitting the ball and holding the stick.

Equipment needed: Sticks, Balls, Cones

Learning Objectives

Students will:

1. Demonstrate proficiency in properly holding the stick (one hand on top and the other hand below).

2. Demonstrate proficiency and ability to control the ball in a static and dynamic position. (keeping the ball close to their body and in control).

3. Demonstrate knowledge of safety rules.

At this point players should be more comfortable dribbling and controlling the ball while static and during movement. Continue to encourage proper techniques and look for opportunities to challenge players in their development.

Lesson 3 Breakdown

Lesson Segment	Time	Description
Lesson Intro	2 minutes	• Introduce yourself and do a roll call (if necessary). Give a brief introduction on Floorball. • Introduce what skills you'll cover in this lesson.
Safety Intro	3 minutes	• Review safety rules (emphasize stick control/keeping sticks below the waist and that players must never be reckless with their sticks).
Dribbling Exercises	5 minutes	• Challenge players in their dribbling. Use commands (whistle) to encourage them to bring their heads up while dribbling. Work back and forth from looking at the ball and finding the instructor around the room (instructor should move around room). • Emphasize heads up play so players can begin to be comfortable moving while not looking solely at the ball.
Game/ Exercise	10 minutes	• Relay Race #1 Note: This is merely a suggested layout. Get creative and feel free to use what you have available.
Game	20 minutes	• Numbers.
Review/ Closure	5 minutes	• Discuss today's lesson with the students.

Relay Race #1

Players will begin by weaving in and out of cones. The next obstacle will require players to dribble 360 degrees around a structure (cones/chair). Players will then weave through cones ending with a shot on goal. Once a participant has completed station #1, the next person on the team may start. The obstacle course can be changed in a variety of configurations

Equipment needed: Sticks, Balls, Cones (chairs if needed), Goals

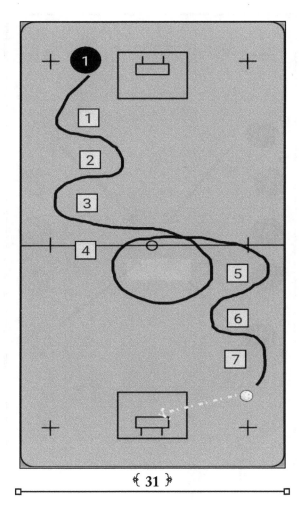

Numbers

Split the group into team A and B (more if needed). Give each player on the team a number (1 through 5), and place the teams on opposite sides of the court. To start use one ball located in the middle of the court. The instructor will call out any combination of numbers they choose. If number 5 is called, only number 5 on both teams will run onto the court, collect the ball, and try to score in their designated goal. Play ends once a goal has been scored, once the ball leaves the field, or after a certain amount of time.

Progression: Call more than one number. This helps simulate game situations, while giving players opportunities to work on skills learned so far.

Equipment needed: Sticks, Ball, Goals, Pennies

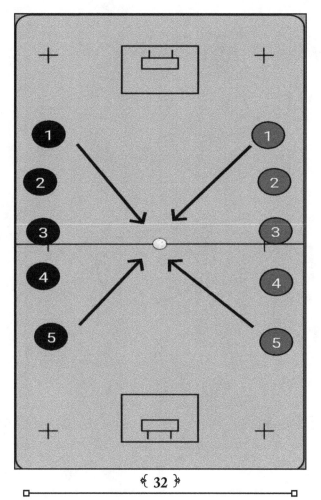

Lesson 4
Passing

Students will learn concepts related to passing (sharing) the ball to (with) their teammates. As a team sport, Floorball requires players to work together toward a common goal to score and be successful. Passing can be a challenging concept for younger players as this lesson tends to require more static movements.

Instructors can emphasize the concept of sharing when teaching passing.

Emphasize the concept of accepting or cradling the ball, when receiving a pass. Many players starting out want to hit a passed ball instead of controlling it and then passing it back.

Demonstrate proper passing techniques reminding players to keep the ball on the ground. The best way to do this is on the follow through by rotating the bottom hand so the palm is facing the ground; if the palm is facing up, the ball will go up accordingly.

Equipment needed: Sticks, Balls, Cones, Pennies

Learning Objectives

Students will:

1. Show proficiency in passing the ball to a peer while standing still with both the forehand and backhand.

2. Show proficiency in accepting (cradling) the ball.

Note: This lesson may cause some more challenges for your players. The concept of passing can be a challenge for younger players, but is a crucial lesson to learn. You may find that your class has a harder time with the activities in the beginning because it is more static. One way to bridge the concept of passing is to frame it as sharing. Most kids understand the concept of sharing and it may help them connect the concept of passing.

Lesson 4 Breakdown

Lesson Segment	Time	Description
Lesson Intro	2 minutes	• Introduce yourself and do roll call if necessary. • Introduce what skills you'll be covering for the day.
Safety Intro	3 minutes	• Review safety rules (emphasize stick control, keeping sticks below the waist, and that players must never be reckless with their sticks.
Game Exercise	7 minutes	• Passing Lane
Game Exercise	8 minutes	• Passing Goals
Game	20 minutes	• Scrimmage
Review Closure	5 minutes	• Discuss today's lesson with students.

Passing Lane

Each player will stand next to a cone facing a partner across the field. Using one ball, players will practice passing to their partner. Players should strive to give good passes to their partner every time. A good pass allows their partner the ability to easily receive and control the ball. Instructors may vary the distance between players depending on the age group and skill level of the players.

Equipment needed: Sticks, Balls, Cones

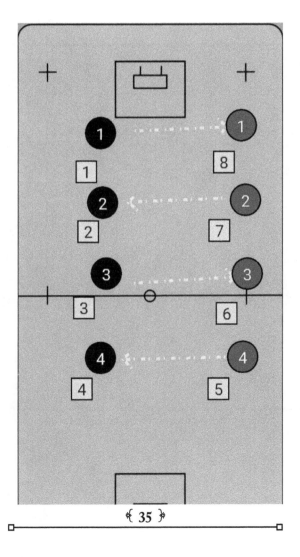

Passing Goals

Each player will have a partner. On the field, there will be a variety of goals (cones) set up. The object is for each player to pass through the goals to their partner, and in doing so, collect one point. Once they pass through a goal, they may move onto another goal. The goal chosen is random and decided by the player who accepts the pass. The team with the most points wins.

Equipment needed: Sticks, Balls, Cones

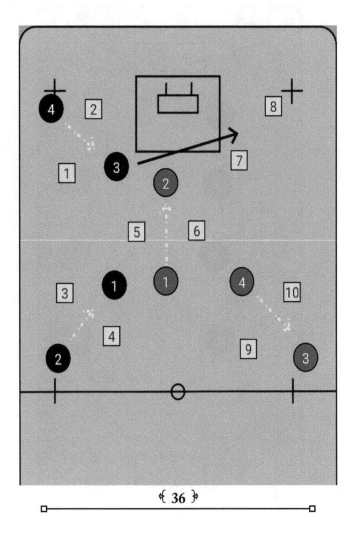

Lesson 5
Gameday #1

Students will incorporate the skills learned in the previous lessons in small area games.

Depending on the number of students, prepare one or two small courts so that as many students as possible can participate simultaneously.

Emphasize player positions and provide a reminder of safety procedures.

Equipment needed: Sticks, Balls, Cones, Goals (or cones), Pennies

Learning Objectives

Students will:

1. Correlate the relationship between becoming a good passer, having good ball control and their overall performance.

2. Be proficient in controlling their stick. (no high sticks, hitting, etc.)

3. Show proficiency in dribbling the ball during static and dynamic movements.

4. Be proficient when passing the ball to a peer in a static and dynamic position.

Game day is a great opportunity to focus on scrimmages. While you may have introduced positions and general game play, this is an opportunity to let students play. If you have a large class, split it into multiple teams and play small-sided games. This is a good time to give them a chance to use what they've learned so far. If you're having trouble with the concepts of positions on the field check out the Airplane Model located in additional drills and tactics section.

Lesson 5 Breakdown

Lesson Segment	Time	Description
Lesson Intro	2 minutes	• Introduce yourself and do roll call if necessary. • Introduce what skills you'll be covering today.
Safety Intro	3 minutes	• Review safety rules (emphasize stick control, keeping sticks below the waist, and that players must never be reckless with their stick).
Game Day	35 minutes	• Break players into teams based on the number available. • If possible, set up multiple smaller fields. • Play short 5-8 min games.
Review Closure	5 minutes	• Discuss today's lesson with the students.

Traditional Field Layout

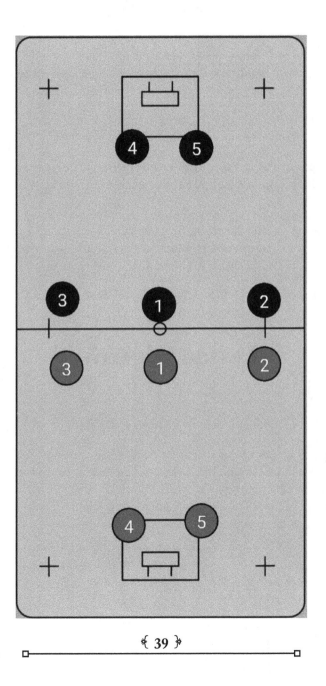

Lesson 6

Shooting

Shooting is not only part of the fun, but an integral part of Floorball. While many new players can grab a stick and shoot, they are missing some of the technical aspects of shooting. In this lesson, the students will learn the basic technique associated with shooting.

During a wrist shot, work with players to start the ball behind their back foot, slide the ball along the ground and release the ball at the front foot.

Encourage players during the release to rotate their palm down and point the toe of the blade at the intended target. This will keep the ball on the ground and straight.

To visualize the process of shooting, imagine the stick as a spring. Load (bend) the shaft as you move the stick along the ground. At the release point, the energy built up will release and help increase the power from the shooter.

Equipment needed: Sticks, Balls, Cones, Pennies, Goals (or cones)

Lesson Objectives

Students will:

1. Learn basic shooting techniques (wrist shot, slap shot).

Everyone loves to shoot but doing it properly can be a challenge. For beginners, watch where they hit the ball. They tend to hit the ball too far in front of their body. Doing so loses power and accuracy; and tends to open the blade up, which causes the ball to rise into the air. One quick fix is to remind players to rotate their bottom hand to the ground on the follow-through.

Lesson 6 Breakdown

Lesson Segment	Time	Description
Lesson Intro	2 minutes	• Introduce yourself and do a roll call (if necessary). Give a brief introduction on Floorball. • Introduce what skills you'll cover in this lesson.
Safety Intro	2 minutes	• Review safety rules (emphasize stick control/keeping sticks below the waist and that players must never be reckless with their sticks).
Game Exercise	8 minutes	• Half Circle • Horseshoe
Scrimmage	30 minutes	• Play small-sided games depending on the size/age of the group. If needed, Numbers game can also be played. • Fouls should be called and free-hits given accordingly.
Review Closure	5 minutes	• Discuss today's lesson with students.

Half Circle

Half Circle focuses on teaching players the proper shooting technique. The player at the end (specific end does not matter) shoots one ball and the rest of the students follow in order. Note: If all participants cannot fit around the goal(s), they can line up in a row and shoot towards a wall. Just make sure there is enough room between the players for safety reasons.

<u>**Equipment needed:**</u> Sticks, Balls, Goals (or cones).

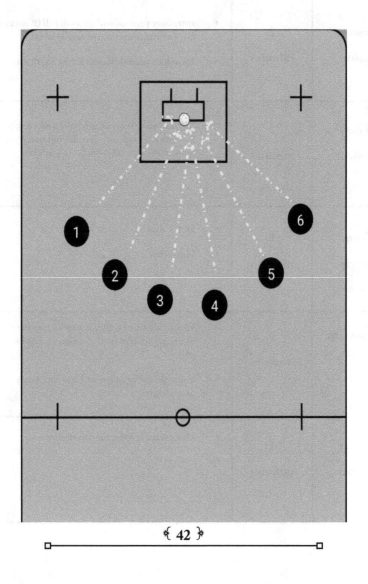

Horseshoe

Player 1 starts in one corner and will run in an arch around the box. Player 2 will pass Player 1 the ball. Player 1 will shoot immediately. The focus is on timing the pass from Player 2 to reach Player 1 as they come around the box. After Player 1 shoots, player 2 will arch around the inside of the box where another player will repeat the same steps.

Equipment needed: Sticks, Ball, Goals

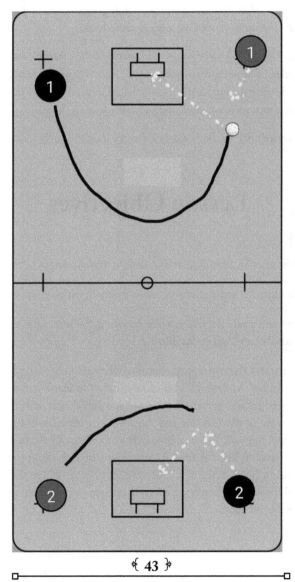

Lesson 7

Shooting #2

In most cases, shooting and passing is done on the move. It's important that players are comfortable dribbling, shooting, and passing while moving. Now that you're seven lessons into the curriculum, your players should have gained more confidence in their skills. If you haven't been doing so already, now is a good time to start putting them into more challenging situations.

Focus on the skills relating to passing and moving. If you haven't done so already, introduce the idea of moving into open space. Typically, younger players have a tougher time with the notion of space on a field. Everyone wants the ball, but now we need to talk about position, and overall movement of the game.

Equipment needed: Sticks, Balls, Cones, Pennies, Goal (or cones).

Lesson Objectives

Students will:

1. Show proficiency in dribbling and passing while moving.

2. Be proficient in the wrist shot (consistently shoot on goal in a static position).

3. Able to run and pass effectively, while knowing the importance of using the stick cautiously (no high sticks, hitting, etc.).

Most kids understand the concept of shooting. They'll likely struggle with the wrist shot in the beginning, because it's a bit more difficult to learn versus a slap shot. For more advanced players, get them to visualize what they're trying to do. A lot of people think you hit the ball like golf; however, the intent is to use the flex of the shaft to propel the ball. Think of the shaft as a spring. By flexing (loading) the shaft you create tension like a spring. As you drag the stick along the ground you create more tension (flex) in the shaft. The release point is where the stored energy propels the ball forward. When done correctly, players will be able to create more effective and powerful shots.

Lesson 7 Breakdown

Lesson Segment	Time	Description
Lesson Intro	2 minutes	• Introduce yourself and do a roll call (if necessary). • Introduce what skills you'll cover in this lesson.
Safety Intro	3 minutes	• Review safety rules (emphasize stick control, keeping sticks below the waist, and that players must never be reckless with their sticks).
Game Exercise	10 minutes	• Pass, Move, Shoot
Game Exercise	15 minutes	• Obstacle Course
Scrimmage	20 minutes	• Reiterate importance of players staying in their designated positions.
Review Closure	5 minutes	• Discuss today's lesson with students.

Pass, Move, Shoot

Players start on one end with a ball. They begin play with a pass to the instructor in the middle of the court. After the pass, the player runs straight down the court. Once they pass the midline the instructor will pass (lead the player) the ball. The player receives the pass and shoots on goal. Players will then collect a ball and get in line to go back in the other direction.

Equipment needed: Sticks, Balls

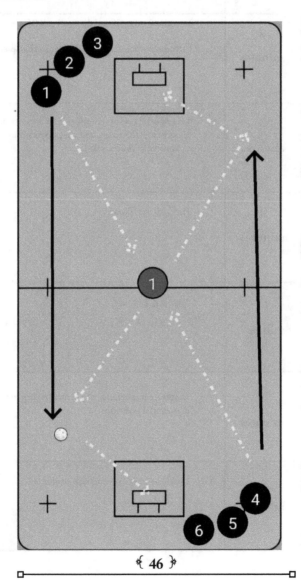

Obstacle Course

Players will work through a dribbling and shooting course. Players will move down the court by dribbling around cones in a zigzag pattern. Players should focus on maintaining control of the ball using the forehand and backhand of the stick while dribbling around cones.

<u>**Equipment needed:**</u> Sticks, Balls, Cones, Goal

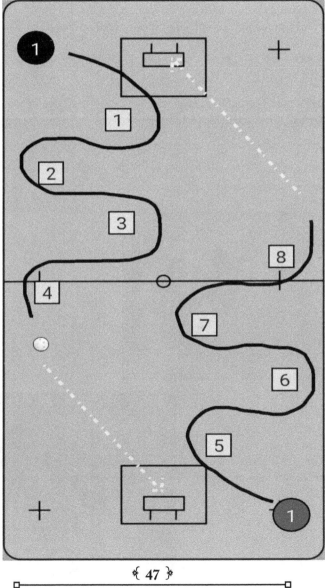

Lesson 8

Defense

Defense is a skill that can normally be overlooked when teaching a sport in the beginning, but the concepts related to defense are an important aspect for players to learn. By understanding how to play defense, players will be able to more effectively play the sport; and will learn specific tactics related to Floorball.

In simple terms, the concept of defense can be broken down to getting between the goal and the ball.

As per the rules of Floorball, a player may not attack their opponents stick to possess the ball; however, defenders may pressure the opponent or may poke the ball away.

Equipment needed: Sticks, Balls, Cones, Pennies, Goals (or cones)

Lesson Objectives

Students will:

1. Learn basic techniques related to playing defense.

2. Learn to play defense without fouling their opponent.

3. Know the importance of using the stick cautiously (no high sticks, hitting etc.)

The defensive aspect of floorball is one specific difference between floorball and floor hockey. This is a good time to remind players about the safety rules. To break it down simply, players are not allowed to go through their opponents stick for the ball. They may reach around the stick, but must contact the ball first. This will be a challenge for hockey players, as it's entirely opposite from how they play. It will take a little adjusting in the beginning. Unless it's dangerous play don't focus too much on calling stick fouls in the beginning. Look for opportunities when a foul happens to call the foul, but explain why it is a foul.

Lesson 8 Breakdown

Lesson Segment	Time	Description
Lesson Intro	2 minutes	• Introduce yourself and do a roll call (if necessary). • Introduce what skills you'll cover in this lesson.
Safety Intro	3 minutes	• Review safety rules (emphasize stick control, keeping sticks below the waist, and that players must never be reckless with their sticks).
Game Exercise	10 minutes	• To emphasize the concept of defense, have players get in front of the ball. The instructor will lightly shoot the ball towards the net. Player will hit the ball away. • Instructor collects the ball and races players to the other end of the field, where players gather in front of the goal. • Reinforce the idea that playing defense is getting between the ball and the goal.
Game Exercise	15 minutes	• Obstacle Course
Scrimmage	20 minutes	• Reiterate importance of players staying in their designated positions.
Review Closure	5 minutes	• Discuss today's lesson with students.

Shoot the Moon

Players are broken into two groups. The object of the game is to hit the cones in front of the goal. Players must dribble with speed around the cone and run to the middle. Once inside the shooting zone, they can choose to use a wrist or slap shot to hit the cone. The first team to hit all the cones wins. If you don't have tall cones then have several goals scored be the determining factor. Think quick, to the middle and quick shot.

Equipment needed: Sticks, Balls, Cones

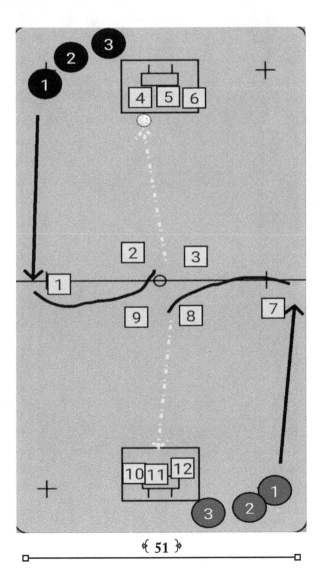

Shoot In Motion

This game can be run simultaneously from both sides. The instructor sits in the middle. Players pass to the middle, then move down the court. The instructor will lead the player down the field with a pass. The player accepts the pass on the run and shoots in one motion.

Equipment needed: Sticks, Balls, Goal

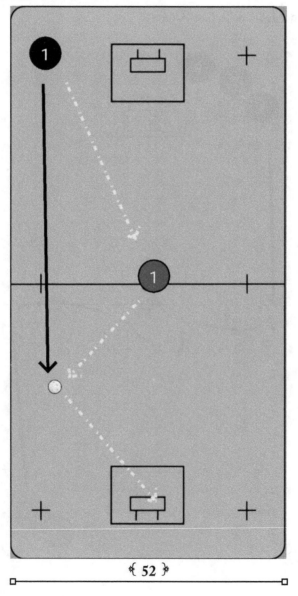

Lesson 9
Putting It All Together

At this point in the unit, students should be proficient in several skills. While there is still more to learn, the basics of dribbling, passing, and shooting should give players a general understanding of how to play. In this lesson, instructors are encouraged to use this time to review previous content, games, and skills.

Instructors should emphasize all the skills learned over the course of the unit.

If there are some favorite activities from previous lessons, they can be used here. It's suggested to ask players what their favorite activities were.

By now, players should have a full understanding of the basic rules of Floorball.

Equipment needed: Sticks, Balls, Cones, Goals (or cones), Pennies

Lesson Objectives

Students will:

1. Know how to hold the stick correctly (one hand on top and the other hand below).

2. Understand the importance of using the stick cautiously (no high sticks, hitting etc.).

3. Move the ball to a satisfactory standard (beginner).

4. Pass the ball to a peer.

5. Hit the ball while in motion.

6. Demonstrate proper shooting and passing techniques.

Lesson 9 Breakdown

Lesson Segment	Time	Description
Lesson Intro	2 minutes	• Introduce yourself and do a roll call (if necessary). • Introduce what skills you'll cover in this lesson.
Safety Intro	3 minutes	• Review safety rules (emphasize stick control, keeping sticks below the waist, and that players must never be reckless with their sticks).
Technique Review	5 minutes	• Cover dribbling techniques.
Game Exercise	10 minutes	• Last One Standing.
Game Exercise	20 minutes	• Four Goals.
Review / Closure	5 minutes	• Discuss today's lesson with students.

Last One Standing

Players start inside a field with a ball (team size can vary depending on number of participants). The goal is to protect your ball while trying to knock out the opponents' balls. If a player leaves the field, or their ball is knocked out, they must exit the circle. The player who remains in the circle after all other players have been eliminated is the winner. Players may not foul another player while attempting to hit their ball out of the field. If the instructor deems a foul occurred, he or she may allow the fouled player to re-enter the field.

Equipment needed: Sticks, Balls, Cones

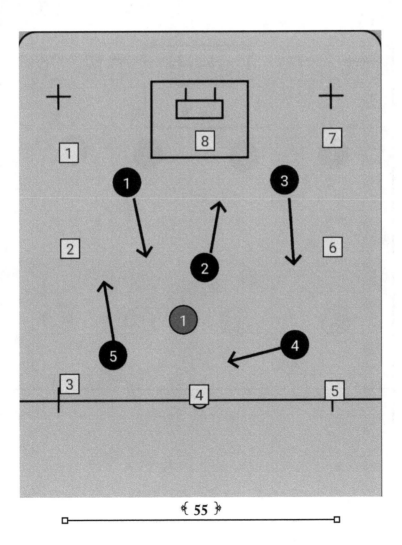

Four Goals

Participants are broken into two teams with two goals for each team. At any given point there are one to three balls on the field. Players must work to score and defend at the same time. Once a goal is scored or leaves the ball field, the instructor may throw in another ball.

Equipment needed: Sticks, Balls, Goals (or cones)

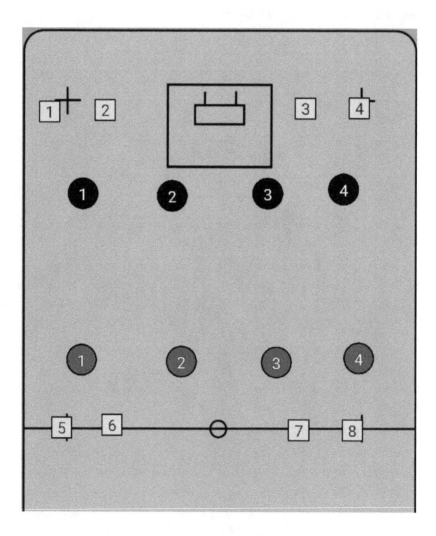

Lesson 10
Gameday #2

As the final lesson of the unit, players should now be proficient in all areas of Floorball. Players should understand basic tactics including positional play, defense, shooting, passing, and dribbling.

Instructors may use this time to review previous content in the unit.

Depending on the number of students, prepare one or two small courts so that as many students as possible can participate simultaneously.

Equipment needed: Sticks, Balls, Cones, Goals (or cones), Pennies.

Lesson Objectives

Students will:

1. Know how to hold the stick correctly (one hand on top and the other hand below).

2. Understand the importance of using the stick cautiously (no high sticks, hitting etc.).

3. Be able to move the ball to a satisfactory standard (beginner).

4. Be able to pass the ball to a peer.

5. Be able to hit the ball while running.

6. Emphasize proper shooting and passing techniques.

Lesson 10 Breakdown

Lesson Segment	Time	Description
Lesson Intro	2 minutes	• Introduce yourself and do a roll call (if necessary). • Introduce what skills you'll cover in this lesson.
Safety Intro	3 minutes	• Review safety rules (emphasize stick control, keeping sticks below the waist, and that players must never be reckless with their sticks).
Game Day	35 minutes	• If you have large groups, split players into multiple teams and use a tournament style of play. Rules of the game, including fouls, should be implemented.
Review Closure	5 minutes	• Discuss today's lesson with students.

Additional
Drills & Tactics

Airplane Model

When talking about positions on the field most adults understand this concept with little direction. They've learned the nuances of offensive and defensive positioning. Kids on the other hand, especially at the younger ages are still learning these concepts. For some this may be the first time they've heard about offensive and defensive positions and may not know what that means. When teaching, try to use imagery to tie in something that they know and understand. Most kids should all know what an airplane looks like, even if they've never been on one. Use the parts of the plane to associate positions. Forwards are the cockpit and defenders are the tail. The fuselage is the center of the field and wings are the wings. Most kids should understand this general layout. In the development phase kids will likely struggle with sticking to their designated positions. They will likely chase the ball because they all want the ball. To help emphasize positioning ask players, "Does the right wing ever touch the left wing?" The answer will be a resounding, "No!" Vice versa for the opposite side. This will help you get players thinking about where they are on the field and begin to instill the concepts of teamwork.

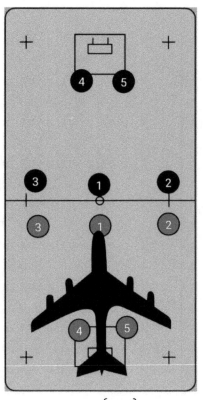

Lanes

Now that you've covered general positions on the field, let's take it a step further. In your scrimmages you should be reinforcing the airplane model. The next week or down the line you can mix it up a bit by using the lane approach. Break the field into three zones using pro cones. The number of players in each zone will depend on how many kids you have. You can have two from each team in each zone or one, whatever works better. The idea is that players must stay in their lanes. There are two things that can happen during this drill. The first is that it shows players visually where their positions are on the court. The second is that it forces players to work together. One player can't dominate the scrimmage because the ball will move in and out of every zone. The concept of passing and teamwork come into play here and can help bring it all together. Players can go anywhere and hold any position at any time. In the beginning phase it's about reinforcement of positions and working with your team to score a goal.

Tips and Tricks:

Don't be surprised if players struggle with staying in their lanes. Use gentle reminders to them about what their positioning is on the court. If you lay it out and it's a mess, stop the group, restate the rules and if that doesn't work move on. Each group you work with varies and some may not be ready for the concept that day.

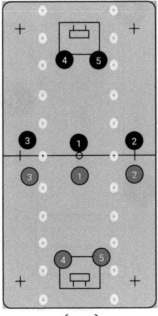

Pinball Passing

Players will pass one ball from one end of the court to the other. Players should focus on controlling the ball then make an accurate pass to their teammate. As soon as the ball gets to Player 3, Player 1 will pass another ball. This will force players to make a quick pass, control the ball, and look for a pass from their teammate. This can be done as a relay competition between multiple teams.

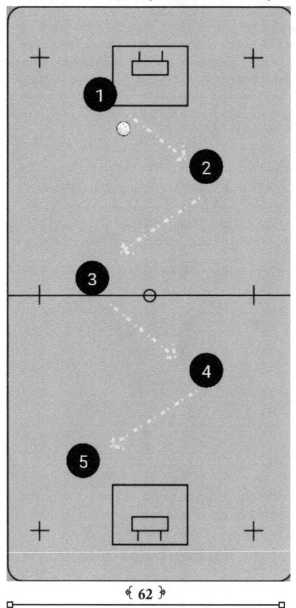

Inside - Out

This drill focuses on players making a quick inside step and then explode around the defender to take a quick shot. Players should focus on keeping the ball to the outside and use their body as a shield from the defender. As they turn towards the goal players should look to shoot quickly on the forehand or backhand.

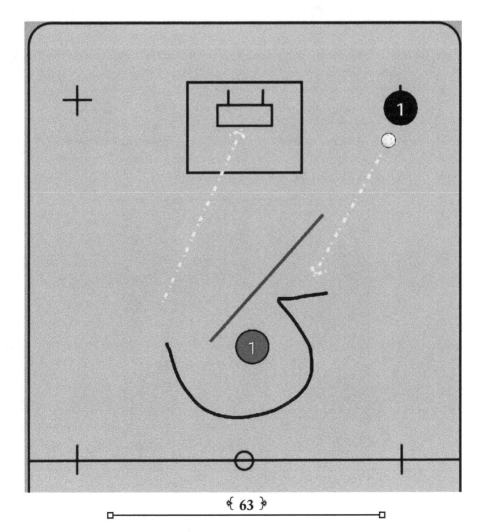

Offensive Options

This is another variation to build from the 2v1 drill. Another adaption you can add is having two defenders as part of this drill. The offensive player with the ball should drive down the wing towards the goal. In this situation they have options to choose from. They can either shoot, drop the ball back to the center who can choose to shoot or pass, or they can pass to the back side. This drill, when done to speed, will require each player to read the play as it develops. Each offensive player should time their runs so that they do not get to their marks early. The key here is keeping the ball moving quickly and precisely to move through the defense. If the defender holds the middle that would indicate they're protecting the pass to the back side. If they don't, the back side is open and the offensive player with the ball should look to pass accordingly. This movement is a routine play in Floorball, and a lot of goals are scored in this fashion.

From a defensive standpoint, encourage players to stay in the middle to protect the pass or shot as best as they can, which is more helpful when working with the goalie. The defender's stick should be low to the ground, making it more difficult for passes to cross through the middle. When playing defense shorthanded, the defender should look to control the ball, or at least get it out of danger so their teammates can recover in a defensive position. Let the goalie handle the potential shot from Player 3 because they will be in better position to do so. It is much harder for the goalie to cross the goal to make a save.

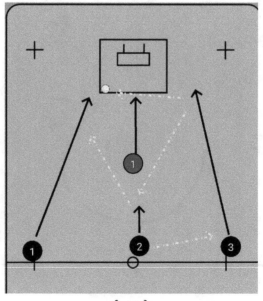

Offensive Movement

When you get a chance to set up a half-court offense there are some options that you can do to create scoring chances. The key is move your feet. At no point should anyone be caught standing and watching. Constant movement creates havoc for the defense as they are stuck watching the ball and searching for where players are moving. If you're lucky the defense focuses too much on the ball which leave open space for high percentage shots. The key is to change the point of attack while being patient. Every pass made must be on the ground and easily controlled. A bouncing ball is hard to control and gives the defense the potential to recover or more effectively pressure the offense. This diagram is just one potential example of how movement of the ball could be made to find scoring chances. Notice that players are in constant motion, and there is the potential for players to overlap and change their original positions. Players must always operate on avoiding a turnover and quick counter attack as well, so they must be ready to jump back on defense quickly.

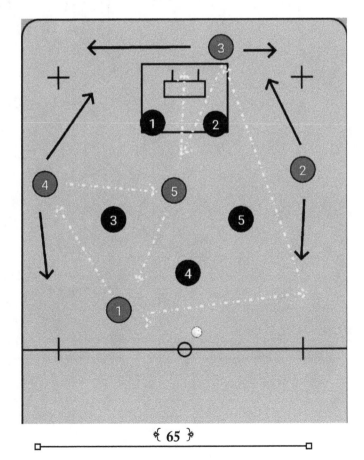

360 Dribbling

Players will attempt to dribble the ball 360 degrees around a variety of cones finishing with a shot. Focus should be on utilizing the top (steering hand) to steer the ball around the cones. During this drill players should focus on keeping the ball on the blade as much as possible. The recommended strategy is to rotate the face of the blade down to trap the ball more effectively against the ground. This will help maintain better control of the ball during this move.

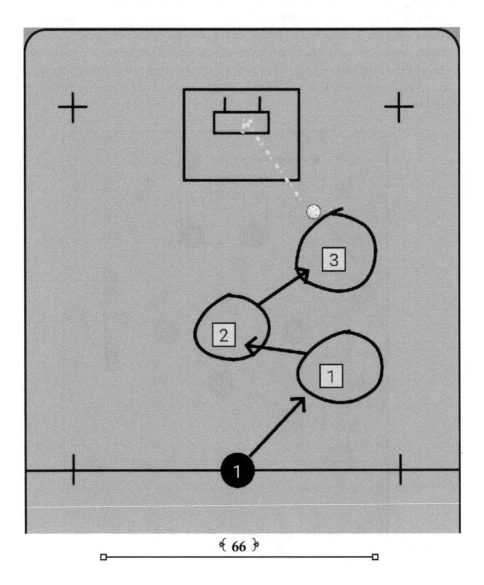

Precision Passing

The intent of this drill is to improve precision passing and speed. Players will remain mostly stationary during this drill. Player #1 will pass the ball from the corner to the middle. The ball will move around the field ending with a shot on goal from the middle.

Progression: Add 2-3 defensive players for game like situations, and to practice powerplay or shorthanded tactics.

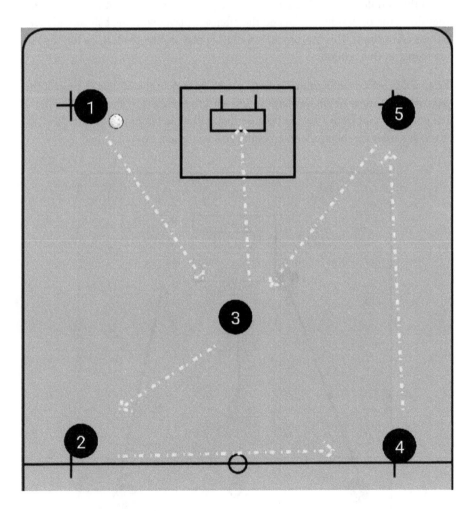

2v1

To start this activity, there should be two lines of offense and one for defense. Whoever is playing defense will step into the defensive position. Player 2 will pass to Player 1 (defender). Player 1 will pass the ball back to either offensive player. At this point the ball is live. The offensive player with the ball should drive down the wing towards the goal. Their partner should be looking for a crossing pass to quickly shoot (note #4 position). Player 3 has options. They can choose to shoot or pass, and that decision should be based on what the defender does. If the defender holds the middle that would indicate they're protecting the pass to the back side. If they don't, the back side is open and the offensive player with the ball should look to pass accordingly. This movement is a routine play in Floorball, and a lot of goals are scored in this fashion.

From a defensive standpoint encourage players to stay in the middle to protect the pass, which is more helpful when working with the goalie. Let the goalie handle the potential shot from Player 3 because they will be in better position to do so. It is much harder for the goalie to cross the goal to make a save.

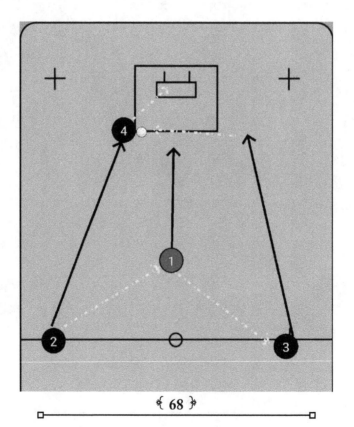

Crossing Patterns

The focus from the offensive standpoint is to create movement. If the offense stays in their lanes they become far more predictable to the defenders. This drill encourages players to cross paths, and change direction, which changes the point of attack. If repeated multiple times, the result could be different each time, thus making it harder to predict what may happen. What's fun about this drill is it forces offensive players to think ahead about what they want to do and then communicate that to their partners. It also encourages players to get creative and have fun, though not always fun for the goalie, but a good one for them work on quick side to side movement. This drill can be done with and without defenders. If using defenders encourage them to not watch the ball, but see the whole field.

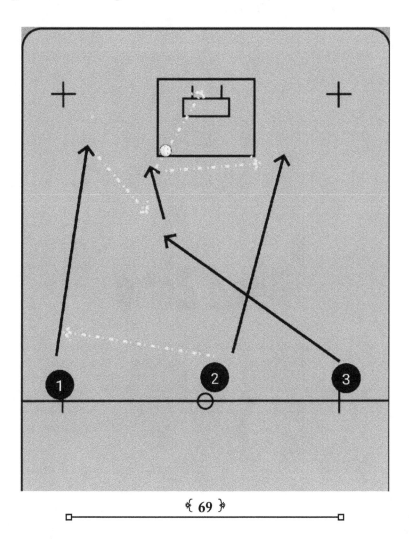

Dead Zone

When you're thinking about Floorball and developing an attacking or defending strategy it's a good idea to break it into thirds. The middle area (dead zone) is one area to take note of. This area of the court is a dangerous area to be aware of. The intent here is to not lose the ball in this area, but to make a concerted effort to protect the ball and move it into the attacking zone. On the opposite side, the defense can quickly use a turnover in this zone to create scoring chances. A team that is unable to effectively move the ball through the dead zone will struggle to create scoring chances and will likely have this space used against them. In some cases, teams may press the offense here so it's important for players to be aware. If needed bring the ball back into the defensive zone and reset the attack. Be careful not to force the ball through this zone.

Defense to Offense

One effective strategy to employ is to effectively transition from defense to offense. In this scenario the ball has been dumped into the corner. Player 1 (blue) would be the closest one to the ball. In this position they have a handful of options they can choose from. For this drill the focus should be on brining the ball behind the goal and then getting it to the center in the middle of the court. Often, we tell players not to put the ball into the middle of the court. However, if the middle is open, then use it. Player 4, as the center, has a plethora of options to move the ball. The goal here should be to get the ball to the wings by putting the ball into space for them to run to. If the ball is placed down the line to Player 5, it disrupts the defense positioning. With the defense focused on the ball Player 3 can cross through the middle and Player 4 can now play the wing. This movement, when done properly can be an effective way to transition to a fast break and can put the defense out of position. It is also important that, as the play develops, that the blue defenders push forward to support the offensive play.

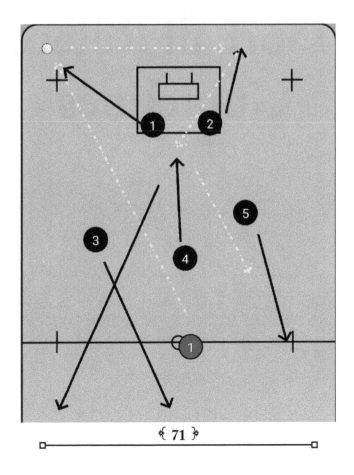

Floorball Referee Guidelines

Role of a Floorball Referee

Development To Expert

Being an official takes a unique and dedicated person to do the job right. Each official is a vital component of the larger puzzle. Without your participation, the formation of leagues, tournaments and matches wouldn't be possible. All officials have a responsibility to keep the integrity of the game, officiate based on the designated rules and ensure all athletes are safe. You can find the entire IFF Rule Book online: http://www.floorball.org.

This information is focused on giving new and developing referees a basic understanding and knowledge of the rules, mechanics, and game management. In many cases officials will be learning the game along with the players. It is important that you are playing Floorball according to the International Floorball Federation rules, and not a pseudo form of hockey. This information will help you get started in officiating Floorball for youth, adult rec, and intramural programs. The rule book used for Floorball is governed and created by the International Floorball Federation. Please note that these rules are designed for official sanctioned IFF events, and at all times these rules should be followed. With that in mind, you may have to adjust some rules and regulations to suit the needs of the league or program you're officiating. Whenever possible the object is to follow all designated IFF rules.

Referee Development

A referee's development doesn't end after they have completed and passed the test. Training never stops and as an official you should continue your learning and development. This training can come in a variety of forms from face to face training events, watching other officials in person and through video. Officiating is a skill that must be developed and worked on over time. It's not something that just happens overnight. Each match will present new opportunities and challenges to grow. You will miss calls and make poor decisions. It's not possible or reasonable to expect a perfect outcome. However, your goal is to be as close to perfect each time you step onto the court. You can't do it alone, and thankfully the officiating world is small, so use those around you.

Referee Equipment

Referees have their own designated jersey and equipment. A referee should always look and act professional. Referees must have a designated jersey that clearly distinguishes them from the other players. It's recommended that officials wear black shorts and knee-high socks. They must also carry a whistle and red card. If you do not have access to a scoreboard, it is recommended that you also carry a stop watch.

The Job of Referee

The job of the referee is to call the game according to the designated rules to the best of their ability. Each situation presented might lead to a different outcome. It is the job of the referee to distinguish the rules and situations accordingly. Above all else, the referee is responsible for the safety of all players on the court and should always act to preserve safety. As the referee you will have to deal with difficult players and parents. However, you should always act in a professional manner becoming of your role as the leader on the court. You have the power to diffuse and control tense situations as needed.

Rules of Floorball

For the purposes of this book we will not cover every aspect contained in the IFF Rule book. We will highlight the key components that you'll likely come across. Depending on available space, number of players, and available equipment, the designated rules may or may not be applicable. Don't stop playing, but do understand what the official rules are.

Hit-In vs. Free-Hit

Two terms that should be understood include hit-in and free-hit.

Hit-in typically occurs when the ball leaves the rink. This requires a player to physically hit the ball into play. Think of a slap shot. If a player slides the ball to put it back into play that is a foul and the ball is awarded to the other team.

Free-hit typically follows a foul and is awarded to the non-offending team.

A hit-in occurs where the ball leaves the playing surface, unless it is behind the goal. In this instance, the hit-in will take place at the corner dot.

Fixed Situations

Fixed situations pertain to an action where play has stopped. Think of it as a free kick in soccer. The non-offending team may choose to quickly restart play, or they can prepare a set play. The offense may not intentionally slow the pace, but may set up a play. Likewise, the defense may not intentionally slow a quick restart by standing in front of the ball. If needed the official may give an initial warning regarding a long delay.

Classification of fixed situations are:

Face-Offs

Face-offs occur after a goal is scored, start of a new period, when play is interrupted and neither team can be awarded a hit-in, free-hit, or a penalty shot. Situations include: damaged ball, boards being dislodged, serious injury, or goal is disallowed (specifically if a foul did not occur as part of the play).

Face-offs should be taken at the nearest face-off dot. If you don't have one specifically designated, do the face-off in a space where one would likely be. Looking at a template of a Floorball field will give you a reference to where the dots are located.

All players, except the two taking the face-off, must be back at least 3 meters.

Goals can be scored directly off a face-off.

Hit-in

A hit-in occurs when the ball leaves the rink, hits the ceiling, or any object above the rink. It is awarded to the team that wasn't the last to touch the ball before leaving the playing surface. In a gym setting without boards you can designate a location on the walls where this rule would apply.

If the ball leaves the playing surface, place it at the point of exit, about 1.5 meters (5 feet) from the boards. If the ball goes behind the goal line, place it at the nearest corner dot.

1. Ball must be hit (think slap shot).

2. Can go directly in goal.

Player taking hit-in may not touch ball before it has been touched by another player or player's equipment. If touched twice before either situation happens a free-hit is awarded to the opposing team.

Free-Hit

A free-hit is taken when there is a foul. When possible play the advantage rule.

Advantage applies when the team fouled maintains control, if through control they have the opportunity greater than a free-hit. If a foul occurs during a counter attack but doesn't impede the offensive team, "play the advantage". In this situation the offensive team has the upper hand to possibly score. Calling a foul would impede that advantage, though not always.

During a free-hit defensive players must be 3 meters away from the ball. Defensive players should do this automatically. Officials can warn players about this rule.

Defensive players should not actively stall a free-hit (example: soccer players hovering over the ball after a foul to slow pace).

A free-hit may be taken at any time, but if it is played while defensive players are trying to take their position play should not stop.

The player taking the hit-in may not touch the ball before it has been touched by another player or player's equipment. If touched twice before either situation happens, a free-hit is awarded to the opposing team.

1. Ball must be hit (think slap shot)

2. Can go directly in goal.

Fouls Leading to Free Hit (fixed situations)

Most common fouls:

1. Stick Checking: player slashing down on opponent's stick. This contact is not allowed and is a good way to break sticks.

2. Stick Lifting: player uses their stick to get under and lift their opponent's stick off the ground.

3. Player lifting stick above the waist during back swing or follow through.

4. Playing the ball with stick or foot above the knee.

5. Player puts stick, foot, or leg between opponent's legs.

6. When a field player is in the goalkeeper area.

7. A field player jumps to stop the ball. Players must keep both feet on the ground. (running not included here) Players may jump over the ball as long as they do not touch it.

In Floorball there are two goalie zones. A larger box where all players may stand in. A second smaller area only for the goalie. Players can move through this space if the official deems they do not affect play. However, they are not allowed to have a body part in this space. Sticks are allowed, but this space is for the goalie. A player deemed in the goalie area during a goal would be a foul and the goal disallowed with a free-hit awarded to the defensive team.

A goalie leaves the goal box entirely while touching the ball with their hand. A goalie is allowed to grab the ball as long as any part of their body is in contact within the goal box. Once they leave the goal box they become a field player and are not allowed to grab the ball. They may play it with their feet.

If a goalie grabs the ball and their foot is in the box, but not touching the ground in the box it is considered a foul.

If a goalie throws or kicks the ball through the air over the center line. If the ball touches the ground prior to crossing the center line, no foul called.

If a goalie touches the ball with their hands from an intentional pass from teammate, a foul is called. This can be situational, and in most cases is at the discretion of the referee if they deem that the pass was intentional.

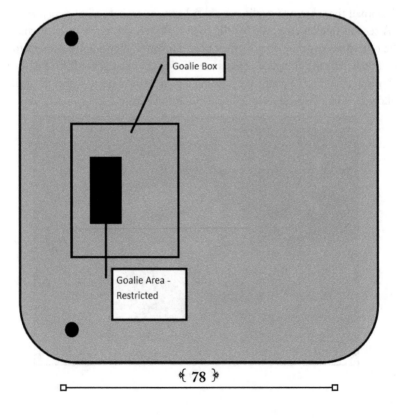

Goals

Correctly scored goals:

1. Considered a goal when the entire ball crosses the goal line from the front of the goal.

2. There must not be a foul leading to a free-hit or penalty.

3. Own goals are considered goals.

Incorrectly scored goals:

1. A player on the attacking team commits a foul as part of the goal.

2. Attacking player intentionally directs, or kicks ball with any part of their body into goal.

3. Ball crosses the goal line after time has run out for the period.

Overview of Mechanics

It is important that all officials understand and continue to work on their basic mechanics. When we're talking about mechanics we're talking about overall presentation, professionalism, and ensuring that the proper procedures are being followed. Understanding and developing your mechanics on the court is only one piece in your overall development. It's an important part of that development, which is why each official should know and understand the proper calls, signals, and movement on the court.

Communication on Court

The ability to effectively communicate is a crucial component. Players, coaches, and other officials should be able to clearly understand what is happening on the court. Like hockey, officials do not need to report fouls to the table unless there is a penalty. However, when a call is made it is important that the call and corresponding signal is clear and concise.

Another equally important piece is clear communication when working with another official. When possible it's best to work in a two-man system, especially at the older youth/adult levels.

Presence

Sports can get heated at times. Remember that one of the main components to the job is maintaining safety of all players. Officials need to make sure players know that they are there. It's too easy to hide for new officials. Have confidence in your skill and ability. When you make a call, blow the whistle with authority and make strong signals. Your job is not to argue with the player or engage with them about why you made a call. Make the call and move on.

Depending on the game, you'll need to step things up a bit. If teams are being more aggressive it will be important that you maintain control of the game through your calls and presence on the court. This is a learned skill and requires confidence in your abilities and a trust in your partners' abilities to do that job effectively.

Signals

Hand signals are an important component to learn and are part of the overall development for officials. Signals help communicate quickly what is happening on the court. Referee signals can be found in the IFF Rule Book. While there are a lot of signals to learn, the most basic ones start with or include hit-in, free-hit, goal, timeout, advantage, and face-off. As officials and players learn these signals and their meaning, it can be helpful to add vocal cues as needed. The key is clear communication, so everyone understands what the call was.

Movement on Court

In a two-man system each referee is responsible for an area. This requires officials to focus on what is happening in their area as opposed to seeing the entire field.

Floorball is a fast-paced sport and it's important that each official be able to see their zone and make appropriate calls. This level of officiating requires a level of trust between the two officials. If R1 is making a call across the court where the play happened in front of R2 that's a tough call to justify. From the position of R1 it may look like a foul, while R2 has a clearer angle on the play doesn't see a foul. Over time, if R1 continues to do this it undermines the team while frustrating both players and R2.

If you're constantly making calls out of your zone that means you're not watching your zone, and not working together as a team. From this position, be ready to move in either direction. Floorball happens fast so be prepared to move immediately after the initial whistle to get into proper position.

Basic Field Movement

Based on the general flow of the game in a two-man system this is a basic pathway for both officials. Notice that this set up will flip based on the flow of the game. How you move on the court will vary, but paying attention to what's happening on the court as well as where your partner is positioned will somewhat determine how you move in relation to that.

If the ball goes out of bounds behind the goal on the far side of R1, the ball will be placed at the nearest dot, and a hit-in awarded. R1's positioning will now begin behind the goal focusing on the hit-in area, while R2 will cover the main area of the field below the center line. Once the ball is played forward R1 will rotate around the goal into the proper alignment path.

As the game progresses you'll come across many different scenarios. Each one will present challenges to make the correct call. Where and how you are positioned on the court in relation to those situations will help put you in the best position to make the most accurate call.

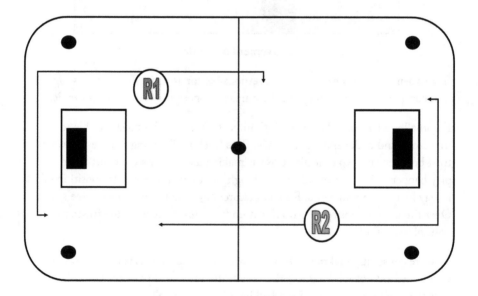

Referee Field Movement

Hit-In from the corner

This is a very common situation in Floorball. In Floorball there is an imaginary line from one corner dot to the other side. It is the same on both ends. If there is a situation where a hit-in or free-hit is awarded behind this imaginary line, it must be placed at the corner dot.

Let's assume that the ball is given to the attacking team regardless of the reason. Defensive players must be a minimum of 3 meter away, including their stick.

Strategically this situation is a scoring opportunity for the attacking team. R2 should be focused on contact with the ball, while R1 should be focused on movement of players across the court. Anticipate a lot of movement from both offensive and defensive players as they jockey for position. Don't get caught watching the ball, specifically in you are in R1's position.

Given the speed of the game, Floorball is built for quick counter attacks. While the play may start in the corner it can quickly reverse the opposite direction. Be ready to move and adjust quickly.

Goal & Time Out

It's important that officials maintain visual of all players, especially during time outs and after goals are scored. Be careful not to rush to report the goal, but maintain visual of players before and after the goal. Frustration comes when goals are scored on the defense, and in a close game, or a blowout, players may react poorly.

Maintain control of the field and create a presence that all players and coaches know that you're in control of the game.

Game Management
Role of referee on the court

Be focused. Focus on the task at hand, focused on making the correct calls, keeping player safe, and doing the job 100%. Too often we can get distracted, and a distracted official is a recipe for disaster. The players, coaches, and fans all expect that you will be focused and give your full attention to the field.

Your body language matters. If you want people to take your seriously you need to be serious. Good officials are present in the moment, professional, and engaged. You may not know it but your body language speaks volumes about you. If players, or your partner, don't think you're engaged how will they trust that you will make the right calls and keep them safe? Be engaged. Have energy. Most importantly have fun.

Communicate. All good referees do one important thing well, they communicate clearly and effectively with players and coaches. When you make a call blow the whistle with some authority. All players and coaches should clearly hear the whistle blown. When needed make sure to speak up and speak clearly. Create a relationship with players and talk to them as needed. Use the players to help defuse situations as needed.

Have an effective pregame routine. Warming up matters as part of your game preparation. It's important the officials be as prepared physically as the players. What's equally important during the pregame is coordinating with your partner and the secretariat to ensure everyone is on the same page. Use this time to discuss mechanics, signals, communication, and to share knowledge about the teams and players. Don't skip on the preparation.

Learn how to read players' reactions. This is a critical skill when learning to manage players.

When a defender makes a hard, fair challenge and takes the ball away from an attacker, the attacker may respond with more vigor than normal and go after the defender. Was the initial challenge a foul? Did you miss the call? Whether that's the case or not doesn't necessarily matter in the moment. However, you likely know one way or the other. Depending on this situation you should be aware of the secondary foul and be prepared to act accordingly.

If you can catch it in time, you can potentially prevent it from escalating by having a strong presence near the players, or be ready to make a quick call. If things get heated it is the role of the official to diffuse it quickly and regain control.

Every game is different and will be presented with different situations. Some games may have more weight to them, playoffs, championships, etc. Be aware of the situation, and be prepared. It may be something as simple as jumping on a hard foul early with a loud whistle and forceful signal. Be willing to set the tone early if needed. The goal is not to over officiate, but to call the game. Players being players will look for an advantage they can get and exploit it.

Refereeing Brand-New Players

Floorball is a developing sport in the U.S. However, most people don't know the sport exists. While it is a hockey like sport, it does have some differences to hockey. Make sure to know the differences. Many schools and universities have floor hockey or hockey programs in place. It's important to make sure that players are playing Floorball and not the latter. The goal in development is getting players to play the game as intended, but you may not need to follow every rule in the beginning. As you learn the rules and flow of the game, and as players develop a better understanding, you can evolve. When starting out get people playing and having fun.

Good place to start:

1. Focus on safety

2. Calling high sticks, stick checking and stick lifting, unsafe play, and body contact.

3. Understanding the nuances of a hit-in and free-hit.

Advantage Rule

With offenses leading to a free-hit, the advantage rule shall be applied whenever possible. The advantage rule implies that if the non-offending team still controls the ball after an offence, they shall have the opportunity to go on playing if this gives them a greater advantage than a free-hit. If advantage is being played, and the game is interrupted because the non-offending team loses control of the ball, the resulting free-hit shall be placed where the last offence occurred.

Conflict Management

As a referee you're going to have to deal with a lot of conflict. It's not enough to know the rules and follow them, but you must have a clear understanding of each situation presented. You will also need to consider that everyone has different personalities and may respond differently depending on the situation.

Control the negative comments - Often you can start to tell when the game is moving in a negative direction. Regardless of what you might hear from the stands, you'll be able to hear what's being said on the court. Addressing language on the court can help reset the players going forward. Give a warning and if needed take it to the next level. Get on it early if needed.

Focus on the current situation - If you're talking to a coach or player about a decision stick to what just happened. Keep it short, clear, and move on. Don't reminisce about what happened earlier and don't let the coach just chew your ear off.

Limit your response - When asked a question, give a clear and concise answer. Keep it short and move on. Getting into a debate hurts rather than helps the situation.

If the game is stopped, get it restarted quickly - It's likely that your judgement of a call will come into question. If it's a judgement call situation do not respond to inquiries that may be made. If a negative comment was made address the comment, move away, and restart the game as quickly as possible. The key is to get the players attention back on the game.

Be decisive in your calls - At all times remain assertive and decisive. Never let it appear that a player or coach's argument over a call swayed your decision to reverse a call.

Check your emotions - Be engaged in the game, but it's also important to ensure that you're not emotionally involved in the game. Keep a calm head and control your own energy, especially during a close or heated game. Take time to slow yourself, and if needed slow the game briefly.

Sample Rule Book

RULES:

- Two teams of 5 players can be on the court for each team. For an official game, a minimum of four players must be present.

- Each match will consist of (2) 15 minutes periods.

- No catching the ball or hands on the ball. The infraction results in a free-hit for the other team.

- No jumping (one foot must be on the ground when receiving the ball). This infraction results in a free hit.

- Players may not go down on two knees to make plays or block shots. This infraction results in a free-hit. (players may have one knee on the court).

- Players may not play the ball with stick or feet above the knee. If contact is made with the ball above the knee: the infraction results in a free-hit. (note: the height is based on the player standing straight up).

- Sticks must stay below waist level when shooting with a similar follow through allowed.

- Stick above the waist on a shot will result in a free-hit.

- No stick checking, lifting, or slashing. A minor infraction results in a possession change, an infraction in a scoring position or repeated infraction results in a free-hit.

- No holding of an opponent's stick, shirt or create a general interference, infraction will result in a free-hit.

- No playing stick between another player's legs. This results in a possession change.

- No body contact, with the exception of incidental shoulder contact, infractions will result in a free-hit.

- No playing the ball with the head. This infraction results in a free-hit.

- Face-offs: Face-offs will be used to start the game at the beginning of each period and to re-start after each goal or if the ball is damaged. For a face-off, stick blade must be on the ground and perpendicular to centerline, feet parallel to centerline ball and the middle of the two players' sticks. Players cannot reverse their grip or hold the stick below the face-off line.

- Play starts with a whistle blow.

- Possession changes: Possession changes occur in the situations cited above. Ball is played as a direct free shot similar to a soccer free kick, where the offending players must be 3 meters away and the ball must be shot or played to another player upon the officials whistle blow with a solid hit – not a sweeping motion.

- Substitutions may occur at any time if as long as it is done in the designated substitution area.

Appropriate Standards

The Society of Health and Physical Educators (also known as SHAPE America), has created National Standards for physical education. These standards define what students across the United States should know and be able to do as result of physical education programs.

Floorball is affordable and can be played by anyone regardless of age, gender, and physical ability. Not only is floorball fast-paced and competitive, the sport also promotes team building and fosters positive relationships between peers. Floorball is not only a sport, it's also a tool designed to encourage individuals to pursue a healthy lifestyle. The floorball community embraces the Long-Term Athlete Development concept and its importance for children and youth.

SHAPE America National Standards

"**Standard 1** - *The physically literate individual demonstrates competency in a variety of motor skills and movement patterns.*

"**Standard 2** - *The physically literate individual applies knowledge of concepts, principles, strategies and tactics related to movement and performance.*

"**Standard 3** - *The physically literate individual demonstrates the knowledge and skills to achieve and maintain a health-enhancing level of physical activity and fitness.*

"**Standard 4** - *The physically literate individual exhibits responsible personal and social behavior that respects self and others.*

"**Standard 5** - *The physically literate individual recognizes the value of physical activity for health, enjoyment, challenge, self-expression and/or social interaction.*

www.shapeamerica.org/standards/pe/

APPENDIX

Dribbling Sequences

Dribbling (stickhandling) is a key component of learning floorball. It's recommended that players routinely practice this skill in a variety of formats to increase their technical ability. As an instructor you can enhance this learning through a variety of drills, which can easily be done at home on an individual basis. Children as young as age two can learn these basic skills. Stickhandling skills can be quickly taught in a variety of sequences, and is a great way to start your class.

Teaching points:

Players must be in their "player stance" to effectively dribble. A good way to visually evaluate players is to look at their body and hand positioning. They should look balanced in every aspect. If the hands are too close or their stance is off, the player will not be as effective.

Floorball sticks are shorter, which allow the player to control the ball close to the body. Encourage players to keep their elbows against their rib cage. This will help force them to control the ball close. Players that are reaching away from their body won't be balanced or have control.

Stickhandling Drills.

Forehand to backhand: Have players hit the ball back and forth while keeping the ball in front of them. Beginners will want to look at the ball while doing this, which is fine during a static drill.

Progression:

Have players lift their head up on command or whistle while trying to dribble. Keep it short, but push them a little.

Heel to toe: Players will start with the ball on the forehand and will push the ball in front of their body stopping it with the toe of the blade. They will drag the ball back towards their feet and repeat. When stopping the ball with the toe, players will need to rotate the stick, so the heel is in the vertical position and the toe is touching the ball. This movement will require players to rotate their top (steering) hand to complete this skill.

Progression:

From the initial movement of the drill the ball will remain on one side of the body. Progress this skill to move around the front of the body. Players will use heel/toe movement in repetition (about five times) in the form of an arc around the front of the body.

Front to back: Have players hit the ball back and forth while keeping it in front of them. On a whistle or command, players will pass the ball through their legs, and rotate 180 degrees to find and control the ball. Players can repeat this process as many times as necessary.

Forehand to backhand off the foot: Have players hit the ball back and forth while keeping it in front of them. On a whistle or command players will pass the ball using either the forehand or backhand to the inside of the opposite foot. For a right-handed player, if the ball is on the backhand, they will pass to the right foot. At this point the player will lightly tap the ball forward in front of their body and repeat the skill.

Lifting the ball: Players will dribble back and forth. As they pull the ball from the forehand across the body they will bring the stick over the ball to the backhand. At this point they will angle the blade (forehand down) to create a ramp. Using the backhand of the stick they will lift the ball back across their body and trap it in the forehand position and continue dribbling. This skill will require the player to move their body to get under the ball. The goal should be to get the ball slightly off the ground. It should not go above the knee.

Safety Rules

Your players want to have fun, but we also want to make sure they're being safe in the process. It's recommended that you remind players regularly about the necessary safety rules. Keep it simple so they can remember them, and come back to them to enforce learning.

#1 rule of Floorball safety – Keep sticks below the waist at all times. It is important to remind players, especially younger ones.

#2 rule of Floorball safety – Keep control of stick at all times. This reminds players that they shouldn't mindlessly swing their sticks around for any reason. This is important because the rules of floorball prohibit most stick contact between players.

In many cases, you'll see incidents happen. It's encouraged to keep reminding players and use verbal commands during play. If it's a dangerous situation stop the play/activity and address the issue. If not, use verbal commands and reminders as needed.

Do you have any questions, concerns or feedback?

Contact us!

Phone: 360-819-7023

Email: david@floorballguru.com

Website: www.floorballguru.com

Author's Note: In this curriculum, we have discussed the many concepts and topics that are relevant to floorball. Although some topics may not be relevant in every floorball settings, there are certain notions that are worth repeating. We can never reiterate too many times the importance of enforcing safety rules such as high sticks, physical contact and stick hitting. The safety rules must always be enforced to ensure that the participants are safe. Local rules should also be established at each facility to address local concerns and limitations.

What about the floorball game and choice of activity? The bottom line is that teachers/instructors should choose activities that are well-suited for their specific group. No matter how instructors choose to set up their activities, emphasis should always be placed on the participants having fun while ensuring that all players get to participate based on their own skill level.

A

B

C

Club 4, 11

coaching 3, 11, 89, 94, 95, 97

communication 11, 79, 89, 91, 95

competitions 30, 72, 100

controlling 4, 13, 16, 17, 19, 21, 24, 28, 31-36, 38-40, 43-45, 47, 48, 51, 55, 57, 60, 64, 68, 72, 74-76, 84, 86, 90, 94, 96, 97, 101, 102

coordinating 11, 95

course 41, 55, 57, 60, 63

courts 13, 14, 22, 25, 42, 47, 56, 57, 62, 67, 71, 72, 80, 81, 83, 84, 89-93, 95, 97, 98

curriculum 12, 28, 54, 77

D

defending 25, 58, 66, 70, 73, 74, 78-81, 95

defensive 25, 30, 32, 34, 36, 58-60, 67, 70, 74, 75, 77, 78, 80, 81, 85-87, 93, 94

demonstrate 32, 35, 39, 43, 63, 100

draw 18

dribbling 8, 16, 17, 21, 30-33, 35-37, 39-41, 47, 54, 57, 61, 63, 64, 67, 76, 100-102

drills 9, 12, 16, 17, 21-23, 26, 28, 30, 47, 69, 71, 73, 74, 76, 77, 79, 81, 100, 101

Dynamics 3, 30, 35, 39, 47

E

equipment 8, 11, 13, 15, 31, 33-35, 37-39, 41-43, 45-47, 50, 52-54, 56-58, 61-63, 65-67, 84, 86

exercises 30, 32, 36, 40, 44, 51, 55, 60, 64

F

face-offs 13, 19, 25, 32, 36, 43, 45, 85, 91, 98, 99

G

H

holds 11, 15-17, 24, 30-32, 35, 36, 39, 63, 67, 71, 74, 78, 98, 99

I

incidents 98, 102

infractions 98

injuries 26, 85

instructors 12, 15, 16, 18-22, 24, 26, 28, 31, 34, 35, 38-40, 42, 43, 45, 56, 60, 62, 63, 65-67, 77, 100

interaction 100

interference 98

J

jersey 84

K

kicking 24, 25, 85, 88, 89, 99

knee-high 17, 21, 26, 84, 87, 98, 102

L

lacrosse 25

leader 26, 56, 62, 84, 89, 96

leagues 83

left-handed 14, 15

leg 25, 87, 98, 101

lessons 8, 9, 12, 28, 30-32, 35, 36, 39, 40, 43, 44, 47, 48, 50, 51, 54, 55, 59, 60, 63, 64, 67, 68

limitations 26, 77, 97

M

maintaining 12, 24, 57, 76, 86, 90, 94, 100

management 14, 83, 95

minutes 28, 32, 36, 40, 44, 48, 51, 55, 60, 64, 68, 98

motion 20, 62, 63, 75, 99

movements 11, 13, 19, 23, 25, 26, 30, 31, 33, 38-40, 43, 46, 47, 50, 54, 55, 57, 62, 63, 67, 71, 74-81, 87, 89-93, 97, 100-102

N

non-offending 85, 96

O

offending 99

offense 25, 32, 36, 70, 74, 75, 78-81, 85, 86, 93, 96

officials 12, 26, 83-87, 89-92, 94-96, 98, 99

opponents 24, 25, 58, 59, 65, 87, 98

P

participant 12, 14, 15, 17, 26, 33, 38, 41, 47, 52, 65-67, 77, 83

partner 45, 46, 78, 79, 90, 92, 95

pass 16-19, 25, 30, 35, 43-47, 53-56, 62, 63, 67, 71, 72, 74, 75, 77, 78, 83, 88, 101

period 13, 25, 85, 89, 98

players 11-28, 30-48, 50-68, 70-81, 83-102

protection 14, 26, 65, 74, 78, 80

R

Race 22, 40, 60

S

T

CPSIA information can be obtained
at www.ICGtesting.com
Printed in the USA
LVHW011958140819
627630LV00012B/770